LET'S GO TO THE
PLAYGROUND

WRITTEN & ILLUSTRATED BY
RUTH WALTON

SEA-TO-SEA
Mankato Collingwood London

Every weekend, we go to the park.
In the park, there is a playground with
lots of fun things to do!

You pull the gate open to
enter the playground.

There is a mini merry-go-round, a teeter-totter, rockers, swings, and a slide.

What do you like playing on the most?

You push the mini merry-go-round to make it spin around.

Going down the slide is really fun!

Do You Know How a Slide Works?

After you've climbed up the ladder, a **force** called **gravity** pulls you down the slide. A force is a push or a pull.

How Can You Go Faster Down a Slide?

The main force that pulls you down a slide is gravity. Without gravity, we would float up into the air! The thing that slows you down on a slide is another force called **friction**. This happens when two surfaces rub against each other. If you wear clothes made of smooth or shiny material, there will be less friction between your clothes and the smooth metal of the slide.
You will whizz down the slide even faster!

Invisible gravity pulls objects together. On Earth, it pulls everything down toward the ground.

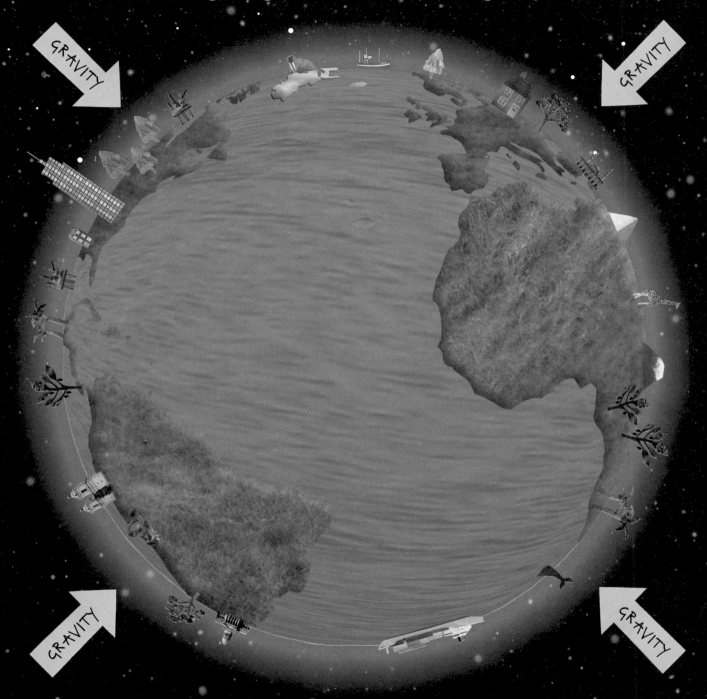

Gravity gives things **weight** and stops everything from drifting off into space.

EXPERIMENT: How Does Gravity Affect Moving Objects?

Two matching balls

Two people

STEP 1: Find a large, flat area of ground, such as a playground or sports field. Look at the diagram below: one of you will drop a ball, and one will throw a ball. You should both let go of the balls from the same height.

STEP 2: After counting to three, let go of the balls. Call out as soon as your ball hits the ground. Try this out a few times, and then trade tasks. Which ball lands first, or do they take a similar amount of time?

Person 1

Person 2

AGREED HEIGHT

What have you learned about gravity?

Check your answers on page 29.

This little girl is playing on the teeter-totter with her brother. They find it easy to lift each other up into the air on the teeter-totter.

Why do you think this happens?

A teeter-totter is a type of **lever**. Each child's weight makes the teeter-totter tilt up and down on a fixed point, called a **fulcrum**.

Take a good look at the teeter-totter.
Where do you think the fulcrum is?

All of these things use levers to help them work:

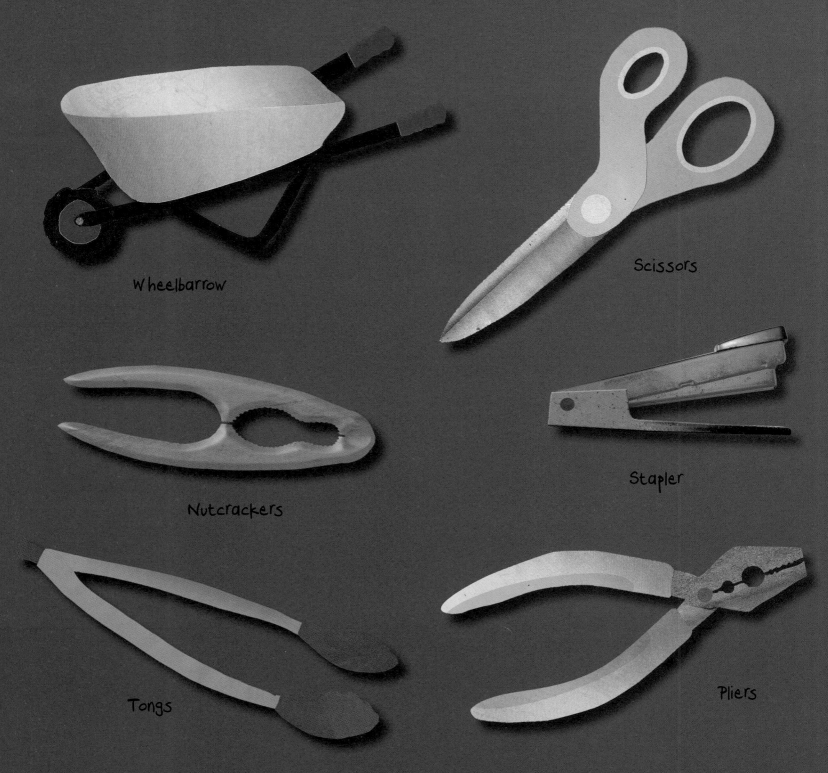

Wheelbarrow

Scissors

Nutcrackers

Stapler

Tongs

Pliers

Which picture is the odd one out and why?

Find the answer on page 29.

cooking on the barbecue

Looking at a map

cutting paper

On the farm

13

Going on the swings is fun. If you swing really high, it can feel like you're flying!

14

How Do Swings Work?

A swing is a type of **pendulum**. The swing hangs from the frame and can move freely back and forth.

Try sticking your legs out while you are swinging. What happens?

15

What Else Can Pendulums Be Used For?

Some clocks use pendulums to keep the time, because each swing of the pendulum takes the same amount of time.

Until the 1930s, most clocks had a pendulum that would swing back and forth, making a "ticktock" sound!

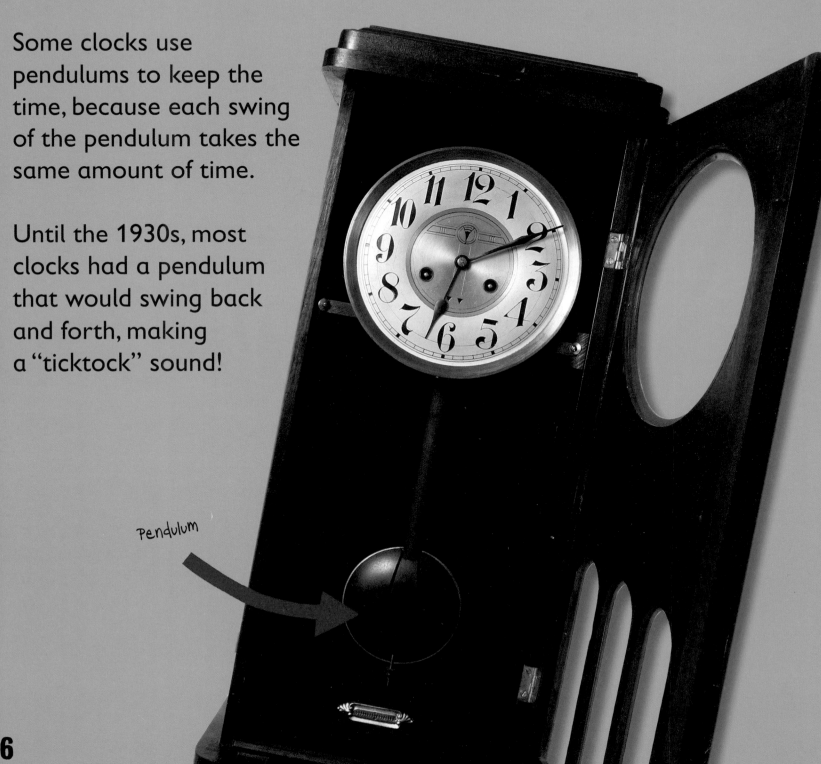

Pendulum

EXPERIMENT: Make a Pendulum!

What You Will Need:

Metal nuts   String   Adhesive tape    stopwatch

A table

STEP 1: Tie the metal nut onto the end of the string. Make a double knot to hold it in place. Attach the other end of the string to the edge of the table using the adhesive tape.

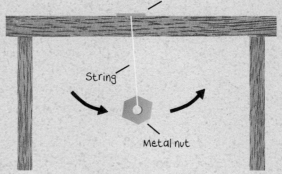
String
Metal nut

STEP 2: Holding the nut, let go of the pendulum at the level of the table top. At the same time, start the stopwatch. Count the number of swings back and forth that the pendulum makes in 30 seconds. Now try timing the swings again, but just give the pendulum a tiny push. Write down your answers.

STEP 3: Add another metal nut and try the experiment again. Does this change the number of swings you can count in 30 seconds? Try changing the length of the string, too! Write down all of the results.

What have you found out?

Check your results on page 29.

If you like to spin around, it's fun to go on the mini merry-go-round. When you are spinning around, it can feel like something wants you to fly off! This is called **centrifugal force** and it works on objects that are **rotating**.

You can go really fast if you get someone to push it for you, but ask them to stop if you are getting too dizzy!

Why Does Spinning Around Make You Dizzy?

When you get dizzy, it is because your brain is confused by the messages from your body. Your body detects motion using an amazing system inside your ear. Fluid inside one part of your ear touches **nerves** that send messages to your brain. When you spin around, it mixes up the messages, so your body feels like it is still moving even when it has stopped!

Inner ear

If you're feeling dizzy, it's good to lie down until you feel better!

At an amusement park, riders on the **carousel** are pushed outward by centrifugal force.

Have you ever been on a carousel?

Riding a carousel.

Don't forget your seatbelt!

When you are in a car and it goes around a corner, you lean over the other way.

What force makes you lean over?

Check your answer on page 29.

EXPERIMENT: Turn a Cup of Water Upside Down Without Spilling It!

What You Will Need:

28-inch (70-cm) string

Scissors

Paper cup

Water

STEP 1: Ask an adult to help you make two holes in opposite sides of the rim of the paper cup, using the scissors. Thread the string through the holes and tie the ends together with a strong knot.

STEP 2: Hold the cup in one hand and pull the string to make sure it is secure. Half fill the cup with water.

STEP 3: Hold the string tightly on the knot and gently swing the cup back and forth. After a few swings, spin the cup all the way around. Practice this outside first!

What has happened?

Check your results on page 29.

Sometimes we go to an adventure playground.
It is very big and it has a wooden climber. There
are many different things to play on.

Which force is
slowing down this
zip line?

What is the force that
helps a slide work?

Take a good look at the adventure playground and try to answer all of the questions! If you get stuck, look back through the book.

Where can you find a pendulum and a lever?

Where is the fulcrum on this teeter-totter?

23

You don't need a playground to play games! Ball games and other sports are really fun and good for keeping you physically fit.

Hula hoops use centrifugal force!

The girl's foot pushed the soccer ball into the air. Gravity will bring it back to the ground again.

Imaginary games are good for your brain and they can be exciting to play.

I'm pretending to be in a jump-rope contest!

Walking the dog can be even more fun if you use your imagination!

What is your favorite game to play?

ACTIVITY:
Design a Playground!

Here are a few things that you might need to make your own playground design.

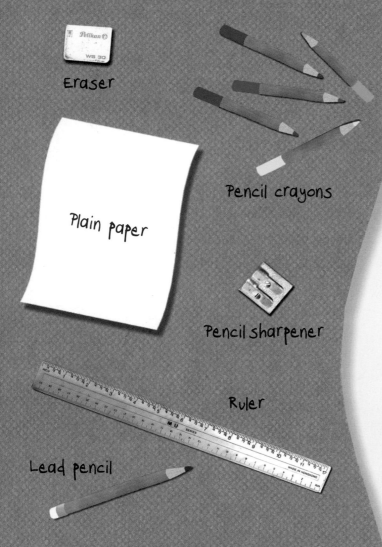

Eraser

Pencil crayons

Plain paper

Pencil sharpener

Ruler

Lead pencil

These pictures may give you some ideas.

Will the slide be straight or wiggly?

What will the climber look like?

What will you swing on?

Will it have a tree house?

What could you climb on?

Don't worry about your drawing, just have fun.
Use your imagination to design the playground of your dreams!

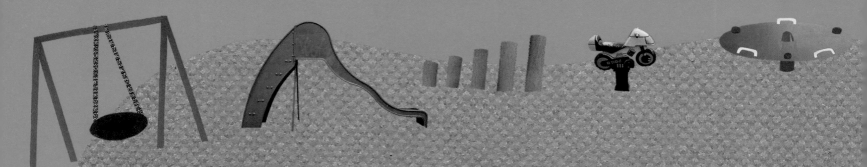

Glossary

Carousel another name for a merry-go-round

Centrifugal force the outward force on a rotating object or person

Force a push or a pull that makes something move or slow down

Friction the force that slows objects down as they rub against each other

Fulcrum the point on which a lever turns

Gravity the force that gives everything weight and pulls everything toward the ground

Lever a bar or a tool that turns on a fulcrum to lift

something or open something

Nerves thin threads that take messages from all parts of your body to the brain

Pendulum a solid object hanging from a fixed point so that it swings freely

Rotating spinning around

Weight how heavy something is

Answers and Results

Page 9: The balls should land at roughly the same time. This shows that gravity affects still and moving objects in the same way!

Page 13: The picture of the children looking at a map is the odd one out. All the others show people using levers.

Page 17: The number of pendulum swings is not affected by its weight or the height of the swing, but it is affected by the length of the string!

Page 20: Centrifugal force pushes your body outward from the circular movement that the car is making.

Page 21: The water is held in the cup by centrifugal force as it spins around!

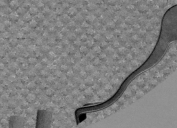

Index

B-C
brain 19, 25, 28
carousel 20, 28
centrifugal force 18, 20, 21, 24, 28, 29
clocks 16

E-F
experiments 9, 17, 21
feeling dizzy 18, 19
force 6, 7, 22, 23, 28, 29
friction 7, 28
fulcrum 10, 11, 23, 28

G-L
gravity 6, 7, 8, 9, 24, 28, 29
lever 10, 12, 13, 23, 28, 29

P-R
merry-go-round 5, 18
pendulum 15, 16, 17, 23, 28, 29
pull 4, 6, 28
push 5, 6, 14, 17, 18, 24, 28

S
slide 5, 6, 7, 22, 26
spinning around 5, 18, 19, 28
sports 24, 25
swing/swinging 14, 15, 16, 17, 21, 28, 29
swings 5, 14, 15, 27
teeter-totter 5, 10, 11

W-Z
weight 8, 10, 28, 29
zip line 22

This edition first published in 2013 by Sea-to-Sea Publications
Distributed by Black Rabbit Books
P.O. Box 3263, Mankato, Minnesota 56002

Text and illustrations copyright © Ruth Walton 2011, 2013

Printed in the United States of America, North Mankato, MN

Published by arrangement with the Watts Publishing Group Ltd, London.

Library of Congress Cataloging-in-Publication Data

Walton, Ruth.
 Let's go to the playground / written & illustrated by Ruth Walton.
    p. cm. -- (Let's find out)
 Includes index.
 Summary: "Discusses simple physics, including levers, and forces, including gravity and centrifugal force, that are present when playing on a playground. Includes science experiments that demonstrate forces"-- Provided by publisher.
 ISBN 978-1-59771-388-7 (alk. paper)
 1. Physics--Experiments--Juvenile literature. 2. Playgrounds--Equipment and supplies--Juvenile literature. I. Title.
 QC33.W338 2013
 530--dc23
                                      2011052694

Series editor: Sarah Peutrill
Art director: Jonathan Hair
Photographs: Ruth Walton, unless otherwise credited

Picture credits: with thanks to istockphoto and shutterstock images.

Every attempt has been made to clear copyright. Should there be any inadvertent omission please apply to the publisher for rectification.

RD/6000006415/001

May 2012